IMAGES
of England

KENTON AND KINGSBURY

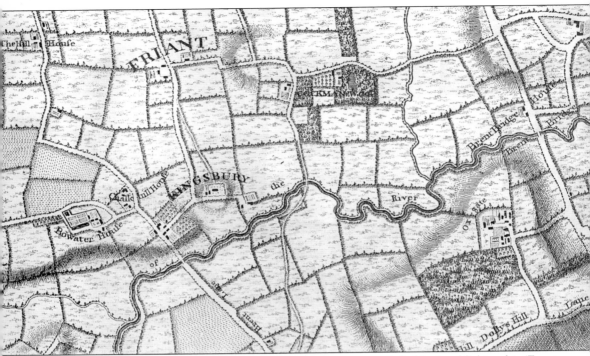

Rocque map of 1746. John Rocque, a French Huguenot emigré, finished publishing his 'Exact Survey of London' in 1746 – it was 16 feet wide and over 6 feet deep! It was the first to acknowledge that 'London' extended its influence well beyond the City's square mile – right out to places like Kingsbury. This part shows Kingsbury as a wholly rural community. There is no Welsh Harp, but the Edgware Road, Watling Street, is clearly shown. All that is left of 'Cockmanswood' is Wood Lane.

IMAGES
of England

KENTON AND KINGSBURY

Compiled by
Len Snow

TEMPUS

First published 2001
Copyright © Len Snow, 2001

Tempus Publishing Limited
The Mill, Brimscombe Port,
Stroud, Gloucestershire, GL5 2QG

ISBN 0 7524 2269 3

Typesetting and origination by
Tempus Publishing Limited
Printed in Great Britain by
Midway Colour Print, Wiltshire

This is for my wife, Joan, whose forbearance and support are of equal measure.

Vater Falls, Kingsbury.   *Reeves' Ser*

The Welsh Harp, formed by damming the River Brent just below the point where the Silk
Steam and Dollis Brook joined. The original line of the rivers is still seen in the boundary line
between Brent and Barnet. Correctly speaking it is the Brent Reservoir, built in the 1830s to
supply water to the then Grand Junction Canal. It has always been known by the name of its
shape – or was it perhaps named after the inn on its eastern shore?

Contents

In *Hvnd* de Gara . tenet . L . archieps *HERGES*.
Pro . c . hid fe defendeb T.R.E. 7 m̃ facit . Tra.ẽ . LXX.
car . Ad dñiũ ptin . xxx . hide . 7 ibi fuᵹ . IIII . carucæ.
7 v . pot fieri . Int franc 7 uilt . XLV . car . 7 XVI.
plus poss̃ . ee . Ibi pbr . I . hidā . 7 III . milites . VI . hid
7 fub eis maneᵹ . VII . hões . Ibi . XIII . uilti qfq̃ dim
hid . 7 XXVIII . uilti qfq̃ de . I . uirg . 7 XLVIII . uilt
qfq̃ dim uirg . 7 XIII . uilt de . IIII . hid . 7 II . cot de
XIII . acris . 7 II . ferui . Pafta ad pecun uillæ . Silua
II . mit porc . In totis ualentijs uat . LVI . lib.
7 qdo recep̄ . xx . lib . T.R.E. LX . lib . Hoc Maner
ten Leuuin die qua rex . E . fuit uiuus 7 mortuus.

Two entries from the *Domesday Book*, William the Conqueror's unique survey of the land he
had conquered twenty years earlier after the Battle of Hastings delivered England into his
hands. Above is the entry for Harrow (covering, though not mentioning Kenton) and below
one of the entries for Kingsbury.

Tra.ẽ . VII . car . In dñio . II . car . 7 uilti . v . car . Ibi . VIII . uilti
qfq̃ de . I . uirg . 7 III . uilti . qfq̃ dim uirg . Pbr . I . uirg . 7 v . bord
quifq̃ de . v . ac . Ibi . I . molin . III . folid . Ptũ dim car . Silua
mille porc . 7 xx . fot . In totis ualent uat . IIII . lib . Qdo recep̄
xx . fot . T.R.E. VI . lib . Hoc m̃ tenuit Wluuard teign . R.E.

Introduction

Kenton and Kingsbury are two neighbouring districts in north-west London, in the modern boroughs of Brent and Harrow. They have as many differences as similarities. For example: both are Saxon in origin, but while Kenton was a hamlet of Harrow, Kingsbury was a parish in its own right. Old records suggest Kenton was in existence first, but Kingsbury claims the second oldest church in Middlesex.

Both were sleepy pastoral tracts – and stayed like that for over a thousand years. Then, like Sleeping Beauty, they awoke to the twentieth century's kiss. Kenton burgeoned in the 1920s and Kingsbury in the 1930s – and spawned its own satellite, Queensbury.

Kingsbury is a precisely defined area – a parish for a thousand years; now, prosaically, that part of postal district NW9 to the west of the unmistakable Watling Street. Kenton can be identified today as the southern half of HA3, but its boundaries are not quite so clear-cut as when it was part of the Harrow parish – without a separate identity but with a specific location, nonetheless.

The territory of Harrow – the *hearg* or temple of the Gumenings (their name is lost, the temple part survives and has changed into Harrow) – stretched from Pinner to the River Brent. Until 1846, it included the district of Wembley which then gained its own parish. It had, for its northern boundary, the road from Harrow to Edgware, known later partly as Kenton Road (or Tyburn Lane at the western end) and partly as Kingsbury Road (or Lane). It went right through the middle of Kenton village. This book attempts to unite the divided parts.

In identifying the sources of the names of the two districts of this book, we are straight away faced with two mysteries. Kenton means the 'enclosure (or *tun*) of Coena'; Kingsbury is 'the king's hunting lodge' – but who was Coena, and which king? I think we can never know the answer to the first, other than to assume he was a local Saxon tribesman who settled with his family by the stream which they may have known by its Celtic name of Lidding. So far as the king is concerned, again we can never know for certain, but a reasonable guess is that it was Athelstan, grandson of Alfred the Great. He had links with Westminster Abbey, which owned one of the two manors that made up Kingsbury. It may, however, as local historian Stanley Holliday states, simply mean 'a holding of the realm', the king, any king, being merely the nominal owner.

In AD 767, King Offa of Mercia – one of the greatest early rulers and a friend and contemporary of Charlemagne – agreed an exchange of land in Middlesex for an Abbot Stidberht. This was 30 hides (about 600 acres) 'between the Harrow of the Gumenings and the Lidding brook together with a further 120 acres on the eastern side of the brook'. This gave Stidberht control over Kenton; there is a reference to a priest's house, which gives us 'Preston'. We can conjecture that his dwelling was further down the Lidding than Coena's *tun*, perhaps at the foot of Preston Hill. The territory of Harrow, which developed into the parish and the manor, came under the control of Canterbury in 832 and remained as a 'peculiar' until 1545 when Cranmer was forced to surrender it to Henry VIII.

Kingsbury developed from two manors, both listed in the *Domesday Book*. The northern was originally called Tunworth and was acquired by Westminster Abbey, later being taken over by All Souls' College, Oxford. The other was owned by Wilfred Wight until snatched from him after the Norman Conquest and handed to Arnulf de Hesdin – later it was in the hands of the Knights of St John, the Freren (brothers) or Fryent as it was known.

For a thousand years, the story of these two districts is the story of rural England: farming, slow to change; a population with little growth; communities centred on the parish church and the manor. Bound at first through a feudal system, this gradually changed to farmers who hired their labourers, but all clinging close to the village.

Change became more noticeable during Queen Elizabeth's reign. Mercantile enterprise, exemplified by Drake and Raleigh, and locally by John Lyon, a founder of Harrow School, encouraged expansion. Lyon and Richard Bowater (of Chalkhill), among others, made money and devoted much of it to their local community. Henry VIII quickly sold Harrow Manor to Sir Edmund Dudley, later created Lord North (not to be confused with Northwick). By a sequence of land transfers, the manor came into the possession of the Rushout family. Sir John was ennobled as Lord Northwick in 1797, taking the name from the family seat, Northwick Park near Blockley in Gloucestershire. Thus, the family seat's name came to be applied to part of their holding in Harrow, as we know it today.

With the Industrial and Agricultural Revolutions – and the accompanying Enclosure Movement – the pace of change quickened. Modern Britain was born. The villages began to swell. First the canals were built (the Welsh Harp was, and is, a reservoir for the Grand Junction (now Union) Canal), then the railways – the London and Birmingham cutting a swathe through Kenton. Then piped drinking water and main drain sewage disposal and lastly public transport created the conditions for the take-off of suburban London.

The first railway to reach Kingsbury was the Metropolitan in 1932 (although the Edgware to Morden Line gave access to part of the embryonic suburb in 1924). Kingsbury was on the extension to Stanmore, later the Bakerloo and still later the Jubilee Line. Kingsbury benefited by being bordered by Watling Street. As one of the main roads in and out of the capital, people who travelled on it, throughout the ages, looked for hostelries, smithies and the like. Gentry could set up their country seats nearby and find their route to London handily awaiting them. Kingsbury was home to a friend of Oliver Goldsmith who came for a short stay to Hyde House Farm on Kingsbury Lane when undertaking some of his writing (Shell Cottage is all that remains of the estate). The Duke of Chandos had his main house at Canons Park, next door to Kingsbury and owned land here. Lord Roberts of Kandahar, one of the great Victorian military heroes, stayed at Grove Park from 1893 to 1895. Other large houses included Kenton Grange (now St Luke's Hospice) and Chalkhill House. And take note of the exquisite Preston Tea Rooms.

Beside the big houses were the farms – Big Bush, Blackbird Hill, Woodcock Hill, Kenton Lane, and Uxendon – all lasted well into the twentieth century. What happened, gradually, and then with a rush, was the sale of farm land for housing development – at a good price. The old hamlets formed the nucleus of the new housing estates at Kenton Green, Pipers Green, Roe Green and Kingsbury Green, and along the main roads. The first significant activity was in the First World War when aircraft manufacturing companies came to Kingsbury (as a sort of annex to the more famous Hendon aerodrome) and changed it for ever. Roe Green Village was built, but completed too late, for workers at these factories.

In the 1920s, Kenton grew apace and in the 1930s, Kingsbury was one of the fastest-growing districts in the whole of London. The old inns were rebuilt; new schools were provided; churches opened to meet the needs of their various congregations. It was a hectic time, creating a new society – metroland in suburbia. Michael Robbins in his survey of Middlesex (1953) slightly ungraciously wrote (after half-praising but not attributing Trobridge's housing): 'Kingsbury merges with Kenton and Stanmore in an unremarkable region of pink-brick houses, recreation grounds, small factories, road roundabouts and bus stops'. There is in fact much more to Kingsbury and Kenton than this, as we shall see here.

After the Second World War, the need for housing was just as imperative; councils took a lead in meeting these needs. Kingsbury, Wembley and Harrow had all started this provision in the 1920s, now it went ahead much faster as Government aid made it possible. Cinemas opened – and closed. Estate agents flourished, as did building firms. Shops stretched along Kingsbury and Kenton roads as well as on the Edgware Road – not to mention dozens of smaller locations, even corner shops. If your particular image is not included, you will appreciate the problem of selecting some two hundred out of the thousands that could have been chosen.

Our history is not over – it never is – but if we stop in the period towards the end of the last century, we can glimpse a past which was exciting for those who lived in it and enchanting for us to look at through the eyes of the photographers who captured it for posterity.

Len Snow
October 2001

One
Introducing Kenton and Kingsbury

It is increasingly difficult, even for people of an older generation, to appreciate that outer London was until quite recently a real farming area. The development of suburbia has been described as the desire to bring the country into the town. Kenton and Kingsbury, though neighbours, developed at different rates. In the 1920s, Wembley (including Kenton) was the fastest-growing district in London; in the 1930s, Kingsbury received that accolade.

One of the most regrettable aspects of compiling a local history is the discovery of how many delightful buildings have been destroyed in the course of redevelopment. The pleasure of finding and recording those that remain goes a long way towards countering those disappointments. Try to imagine, as you walk along (for example) Fryent Way, that you are treading a footpath between fields of hay, with warm farmhouses in the distance across the meadows. Another picture in your mind as you stroll up Kenton Lane might bee the village inn you have just left, set back on the green. It was a serenely different world which the imagination struggles to recreate, until images such as those in this and succeeding chapters reproduce pictures of structures and places that no longer exist.

Kingsbury from the air. In 1962, this is where Kingsbury and Kenton meet – Kingsbury Circle, in the middle left, with Kingsbury Road to the right and Kenton Road to the left. Kingsbury Swimming Pool, now demolished, is the rectangular white shape in the middle. In the foreground, Fryent Open Space, once farm lands, was saved from development as parkland by Middlesex County Council in 1936-38.

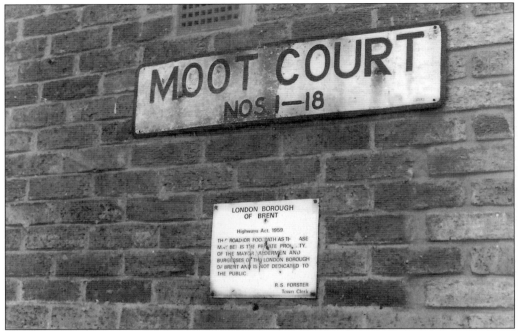

The Moot of the Hundred of Gore. The County of Middlesex was, in Saxon times, divided for administrative purposes into six 'hundreds'. Gore Hundred (in Anglo-Saxon, *Gara*) included Kingsbury and Harrow (and thus Kenton). Its meeting place (The Moot) was a triangular-shaped field, hence 'gore', and it is remembered in the names of these two council-built estates on Fryent Way (and that name recalls one of the two Kingsbury Manors).

Kenton Lane Farm, from a painting in 1811, when the house was fairly new. The painting is by Jane Loudon, daughter-in-law of the famous landscape designer of the early nineteenth century, J.C. Loudon. This was for many years the headquarters for Jack Brazier's dairy, which supplied much of Kenton, Harrow and Wembley. Sad to relate, it is now (in 2001) empty. In its heyday about 3,000 gallons of milk would arrive there for bottling (their own fields and the cows had long gone).

One of the founding fathers of modern Harrow. Alderman W.R. Cowen OBE was the Charter Mayor of Harrow when it received Borough status in 1954. He was initially a Kenton councillor.

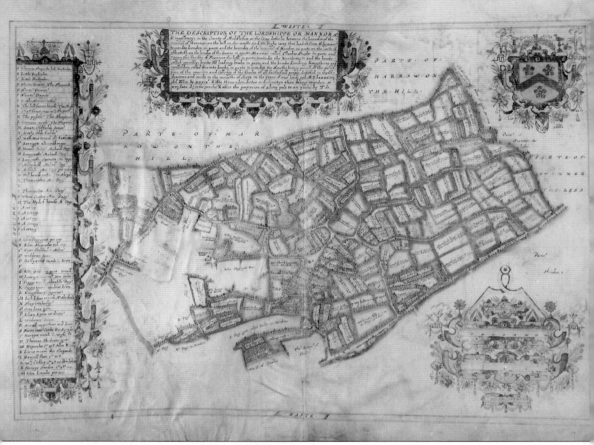

The All Souls' Map of Kingsbury. This exquisite map, dated 1597, was drawn for Richard Hovenden, Warden of All Souls College in the last years of Queen Elizabeth I's reign to show the college's land holdings in the Kingsbury manors. The way the map is printed, Edgware Road runs along the bottom.

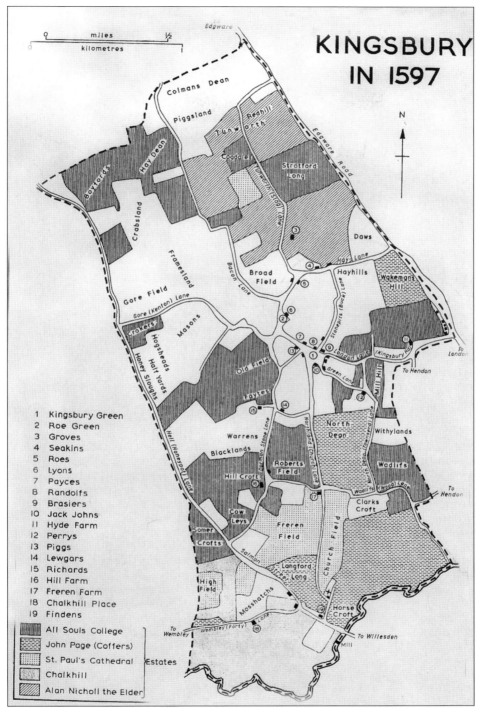

Kingsbury in the late Tudor period. This modern interpretation of the fields and farms is from the Victoria County History and is to be read in conjunction with the map opposite. You can identify, for example, Hyde Farm, Lewgars, Kingsbury Green and Roe Green.

Kingsbury Green in the 1930s. This is the junction of Church Lane and Kingsbury Road; the district council offices were in the white house, The Grange, top right. Kingsbury Road crosses from left to right in the middle of the picture. It is interesting that there is no vehicular traffic to be seen – people walk freely on the road or across the green. Here is the first of Kingsbury Council's familiar gas street lamps. The rebuilt Plough Inn is top left. Soon after this picture was taken Kingsbury snuggled up to Wembley Council, thirty-five years after dramatically splitting from the previously united council. José Diaz (1840-1915) was elected to Kingsbury Council in 1904. He was a descendant of Spanish Hidalgo nobility and he retained his Spanish nationality for some years while still a Kingsbury councillor. He even became chairman, serving there for about ten years (becoming naturalized) and was involved from time to time in a number of stormy incidents, often clashing with Dr Arthur White. He was a county councillor and JP. He and his wife lived at Ferndene near the Green Man inn. It had been built in place of a Victorian house but was demolished in the 1960s. Now occupying this site is an award-winning block of flats, built by Clifford Wearden and Associates in 1966-67.

Kingsbury Green. The scene is summery – how green it was, literally. Buck Lane houses are peeping through on the right.

Westfield Lane, behind the busy Kenton Road. This backwater, as seen in the 1970s, shows the bridle lane at the top end of Westfield Lane – it is still rather untidy. At the lower end is the charming Swaminarayan Temple (see Chapter Eight).

This used to be Kingsbury Lane, one of two roads so called, but later became Black Pot Hill, now Blackbird Hill. The setting is the foot of the hill where the River Brent is crossed by the road to London. The leafy lane was widened in 1923 to accommodate traffic to the British Empire Exhibition. On the right was to be the site of Godfrey Davis' motor showroom (now, in turn, demolished for a new owner).

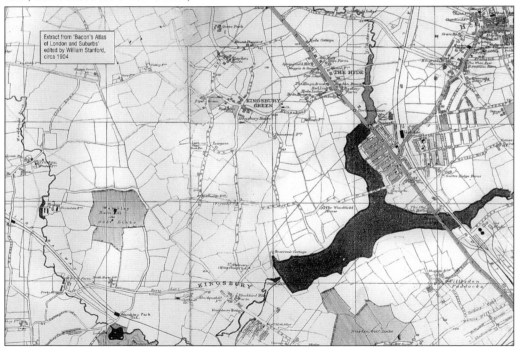

This really is a map to treasure: Bacon's Atlas of London and Suburbs (published by Stanford's), *c.* 1904. No Wembley Stadium, no housing estates, no Metropolitan extension through Kingsbury to Stanmore, but there is a Wembley Park, at the foot of the map – a large amusement park with a boating lake, giant slide, golf links and, later, horse racing. The farms of the period stand out: Gore Farm, Lyon, Kenton Grove, Bush and houses like Grove Park, Lewgars and Hyde.

The London to Birmingham was the first trunk railway in Britain when it opened in 1837. It passed through Willesden and Wembley before reaching Kenton on its way to Wealdstone and Watford. This shows the still wholly rural scene, looking south towards the bridge over the railway at Kenton Road (then called Tyburn Lane) in the distance and Harrow-on-the-Hill on the right.

The third Lord Northwick (1811-1888), by Frederick Sargent. His family had come into possession, in the mid-seventeenth century, both of the Northwick estate in Gloucestershire and the Manor of Harrow which included the local area we know as Northwick Park. His father, the second baron, had lived more frequently in the Harrow estate, but had caused animosity among his tenant farmers, who included Anthony Trollope's father. George Rushout-Bowles (that was the family name) married Augusta Warburton (her second marriage) and when he died, she married Edward Spencer-Churchill. His grandson Edward George inherited the estate in 1912. (By courtesy of the National Portrait Gallery, London)

Sudbury Court Farm, in its last days in 1956, just before demolition. It was part of the Harrow Manor and the principal seat of the Lords of the Manor; thus it came into the ownership of the Northwicks. Some of this building dated back to the seventeenth century – yet another historic building that has fallen to the unstoppable march of the developer. Originally part of the lands of the Archbishop of Canterbury, by the eighteenth century it was in the hands of the Perrin family (who also came to own the former John Lyon farm in Preston). Kenelm Close (whose name tells yet another story; he was a young Saxon King, murdered by his stepsister) was one of the roads built here.

Two

Before the Builders
Arrived

As the Domesday Book *extracts reveal, Kingsbury had two manors. One of these was Tunworth, held by Westminster Abbey, which was bought by All Souls' College, Oxford, in 1439 (under Archbishop Chichele). The other came to be known as Freren (or Friant, Fryent and other variations) from the brothers of the Order of St John. At the Dissolution, it went to St Paul's. Despite these connections and even with its apparent royal link, its proximity to the Edgware Road (the old Roman Watling Street) did not give it any opportunity to link up to the outside world. Until the end of the nineteenth century it remained a total backwater, near the edge of London. It was only the onset of the suburban revolution in the 1920s that changed Kingsbury into a modern setting. The hub of Kingsbury – quite a large parish – was the road that came to link the old church of St Andrew's with the one that replaced it for a while, Holy Innocents.*

Church Lane at its junction with Wood Lane, *c.* 1920. This artistic photograph of a historic site shows the oak tree which flourished where the George Inn now stands.

Buck Lane at the junction with Kingsbury Road. It was a medieval lane, where some Roman remains have been found. The cottages were built in 1825 and were at the heart of the village around the green. The photograph above is probably from the early 1900s. The veteran photographer, Kuno Reitz, captured the scene on the right looking up the hill in the 1920s. The

cottages have long since been demolished and on the eastern side Kingsbury Council's first council housing, Highmeadow Crescent, was built in 1924. At the top of the steep hill are many buildings associated with Ernest Trobridge, as described in Chapter Three.

Big Bush Farm, Kingsbury. This was farmland, hay farming in the main, for hundreds of years. The first photograph in 1928 and the second from 1930 shows it a few years before Middlesex County Council boldly acquired all the Fryent Open Space – though some farming was allowed to continue for a number of years after the end of the Second World War. The farm's entrance was on what used to be called Dorman Stone Lane, now Salmon Street. It was occupied in the early twentieth century by William and Walter Williams, whose family were manufacturers of Idris Mineral Waters – an appropriately romantic Welsh name. It was demolished before the Second World War.

This is one of a trio of illustrations of the rise and fall of one of our most charming old farmhouses, Black Bird farm, Kingsbury. The upper yard was depicted by the well-known local artist C.C. Downer, in 1922. The farmhouse can be traced back to the fifteenth century. At one stage, it seems to have been known as Black Pot Farm.

Black Bird Farm, still in use in 1948, though farming had stopped. The building was pulled down in 1958. The local paper, the *Wembley News*, reported the controversy over the proposal to pull it down in order to build a pub – which did happen. The Blackbirds now welcomes (or did until the stadium closed for rebuilding) many football fans on their way to Wembley.

Farmhouse on Blackbird Hill, in 1926. Just one more old farm building, possibly Tudor, which succumbed to the pressures for change.

This weather-boarded cottage was in the little village of Preston, pictured as recently as 1933 by the well-known local photographer, Kuno Reitz.

Hay making at Pipers Green, 1930s. Hay was one of the staple crops in this part of London (although Hay Lane may not be derived from this apparently obvious root). The house in the background is a Trobridge house, Elmstead, built in 1921, but now sadly demolished.

Kingsbury station in 1900. It was more correctly called 'Kingsbury and Neasden' – still the Metropolitan Line – on Neasden Lane; now it is just named Neasden, on the Jubilee Line. The horse-drawn cabs stand ready to pick up their fares and take them to their houses in Neasden or Dollis Hill.

Depicting a scene in Preston during the 1930s, this postcard was sent about ten years later to his son by the owner of Sherwood's garage, which is on the right – a wartime reminder of the once bucolic scene. The Lidding Brook runs under the road in the middle of the picture, probably flooding every winter until action was taken to prevent it (see Chapter Nine).

This is Hillside Farm (now recalled by Hillside Close) on Preston Hill, just below the Preston Tea Rooms. In the mid-nineteenth century it was also the Rose and Crown beer shop, run by John Walker (no, not the whisky person!).

The Preston Tea Rooms. What a picture that conjures up of the 'typical country village' ready for the townies to relax in – yet only ten miles from Charing Cross. The tea rooms were at the top of Preston Hill at its junction with Preston Road. George Timms ran them from about 1880. As you sipped your tea and munched your scones you would have enjoyed a charming view across the Lidding valley, with Hillside Farm and Uxendon Manor nearby and the slopes of Barn Hill rising on the other side of the little river. The houses on the far right are 356-358 Preston Road. Sadly, Preston House, where the tea rooms were opened, was pulled down for the development of flats in 1962-63.

Cottages in Roe Green. These two were in Stag Lane, opposite Haydon House, as seen around 1920, with Kingsbury Council's standard-style gas lamp ready to light the way for evening travellers or the farm workers shown here. By the 1980s the whole of the junction of Hay Lane and Stag Lane had been rebuilt with flats – Cherry Tree Court, Kenwood Court and Haydon Court.

This cottage at Roe Green had survived from Tudor times at least until 1935 when this picture was taken. It is now the site of the caretaker's house for Kingsbury High School annexe. The biblical quotation, portrait plaque and hanging baskets give a personal 'feel' to the house.

Demolishing cottages at Roe Green: this is the sad face of the developing suburbs – the old gives way to the new and this is how it happened.

Salmon Street in 1934. The style of a country lane has largely been maintained until today; the road is flanked by good quality houses and covered with speed humps. Luckily, the lonely car (an Austin 7) is able to speed on regardless. (From the Wembley History Society – the Kuno Reitz collection)

The John Lyon Farm, spring 1934. It is named after the yeoman-farmer who owned a large area of land here in the sixteenth century and was one of the founders of Harrow School. After his death in 1592, the house and lands were used as an endowment to help fund the school. Tuition was free for the sons of the local farmers at that time. The house was rebuilt in the late seventeenth century and it eventually came to the Perrin family, who in turn bequeathed it to Wembley Council who demolished it in 1960, to build John Perrin Place. They chose that name rather than John Lyon because of the bequest. (From the Wembley History Society – Kuno Reitz collection)

Woodcock Hill Farm dates back at least to the seventeenth century; it stood on 170 acres of farmland. It came into the hands of the Kinch family (they also had land in Preston – hence Kinch Grove) who sold it to Costins for housing development after Thomas Kinch (born in 1869) died in 1954. It was demolished in 1958.

Sheepcote Farm has its origins in medieval times. Its large acreage gave us the Northwick Park Golf Course and then the Harrow Technical College (now University of Westminster) and Northwick Park Hospital – to say nothing of the Harrow School 'Ducker'. It was the home of Thomas Grimwade who patented a type of desiccated milk used by troops in the Crimean War. Florence Nightingale said she 'had tasted the milk product, pure or mixed with food, and found it to be the best substitute for fresh cow's milk'.

Stag Lane, near Grove Park Mansion. This picture is from the Walton Collection, made by one of the family who lived there at the turn of the last century. The kitchen garden is on the left and the polo ground on the right.

The Lodge to Grove Park Mansion, which existed in Stag Lane until the building of Roberts Court.

The east front of Grove Park Mansion, showing a perfectly grand, ivy-covered, Victorian country house. In 1276, a Richard Grove held this land and his name has survived since then, though ownership has changed many times. By the latter part of the nineteenth century, the Walton family owned it and Lord Roberts of Kandahar came to live here from 1893 to 1895. During the First World War its grounds were used as a landing field and the Aircraft Manufacturing Company (Airco) used the house for offices. Between 1923 and 1939, it was a boys' preparatory school (see Chapter Eight) and it was demolished after the Second World War. On the Stag Lane frontage stands Roberts House, a home for older people, and two special schools – Grove Park and Hay Lane.

Polo match at Grove Park Mansion, c. 1900.

Lord Roberts of Kandahar, by G.F. Watts, 1898. Frederick Sleigh Roberts (1832-1914) joined the Indian Army in 1851, won the VC in the Indian Mutiny and became famous for his march to relieve the beleaguered city of Kandahar. He left India in 1893 and came to Kingsbury, becoming during his time there a well-liked member of the community, but then went to Ireland on Government duty. 'Bobs', as he was known, was called to help Kitchener in the Boer War, as his Chief of Staff (sadly his only son was killed there). He was Field Marshal, an Earl and Commander in Chief. (Courtesy of the National Portrait Gallery, London)

Laying tramlines in Edgware High Street, 1904. If I am a little cheeky in including this scene, as it is strictly speaking about half a mile away from Kingsbury, my excuse is that it shows exactly what was happening along the whole stretch of that road where it formed the Kingsbury border with Hendon, a little further south. The creation of the tramway network helped open up the suburbs just as the tube extensions did twenty and thirty years later. Was the policeman keeping law and order or just directing traffic?

Three
Places Here – and Gone

Ernest George Trobridge, born in Belfast in 1884, trained as an architect (he was also inspired by the work of the philosopher, Swedenborg) and came to London in 1908. He and his family settled in Kingsbury at the beginning of the First World War and at the end of the war began both building houses (largely in Kingsbury but also in Colindale, Purley and other sites) and inventing new ways of using building materials. Trobridge patented a form of compressed green elm-wood. Many of the houses were beautifully thatched and he devised a sprinkler system to contain any fire risk. He was an outstanding architect who worked mainly in the twenties and thirties of the last century. Many of his houses are still in use. He also built four 'follies' at the top of Buck Lane. He died in 1942.

Picture postcard of a Trobridge House, 'Simbo'. On the back of the card is a sketch map, used by the owners to show visitors the location of this charming house on Stag Lane. It could be reached by a No. 8 bus to Roe Green from Colindale Station and Oxford Circus. The house, now named Rose Cottage, stands at 351 Stag Lane.

A Trobridge cottage, in Stag Lane. This was part of the proposed Elmwood estate.

Hayland. This was Trobridge's first house to be made from compressed greenwood – his invention. It was built in 1921 and stood in Stag lane, costing £775 to purchase.

It may have been smelly, but it was a part of life – the new sewage farm for Wealdstone in 1907, at Kenmore Avenue. H. Walker was the District Engineer and Surveyor responsible and the building work was contracted to H.W. Pettit of Graham Road. The site is now a Harrow Council Depot – that's what happened to most of these small waste disposal works. They caused so much offence in the neighbourhood that lawsuits were often taken – often by one council against another, and they were taken out of use and other means for disposal of sewage found.

Kenton Road, 1960. A confident, by now well-established, suburb. The telephone exchange is on the right (now closed) and St Mary's church can be seen in the distance. The scene is empty of the hectic traffic, parked cars, noise and fumes of today.

Kingsbury Manor was built in 1899 in Roe Green Park (as it now is called) for the Duchess of Sutherland. It is not clearly visible from the main road, a little haven in the country. Its coach house was used by John Logie Baird to set up his workshop for his new television invention (see Chapter Nine).

Kenton Recreation Ground, 1960s. A charming open space, protected from the ravages of would-be developers for the perpetual use of the local people and still a haven of rest.

Harrow Golf Clubhouse, Preston Road, 1914. The golf course (also called Preston Golf Club) was created in 1912 near Preston Road station. Yet again, the unstoppable urge to build housing estates persuaded the club to sell out and by the 1930s it was built over.

Harrow Masonic Centre and Northwick Park Circle. When, in 1912, Edward Spencer Churchill, the owner of Harrow Manor (which included the area now known as Northwick Park), decided to develop part of his lands for superior housing, he was delayed by the onset of the First World War. However, the middle of the site became a recreation area known as the Palaestra; this in turn became the prestigious Northwick Park Tennis Club. Then in 1934 its pavilion became, and remains, the headquarters of the Harrow District Masonic Association. The aerial picture shows Northwick Circle with the Centre in the middle and side roads like Upton Gardens in the forefront.

The River Lidding at Preston, 1931. Also known as the Wealdstone Brook, its flooding caused a lot of havoc for so small a river, until curbed by persistent work of the river authority. It is likely that the priest who gave his name to the village (Preston means 'priest's dwelling place') lived near the river. The river's original name is Celtic in origin, as with many such names in England – the Thames is another.

Lewgars was on the site of an old farmhouse. In the nineteenth century, E.N. Haxell rebuilt it extravagantly with a mix of Gothic, Tudor and other styles. It was described as 'looking like a cross between Dracula's Castle, St Pancras station and a building in Kew Gardens'. The bell tower was taken from old St Andrew's church. It is another of the charming 'lost' buildings, having been demolished in 1952. All that remains is the road, Lewgars Avenue.

'The Ducker', Harrow School's swimming pool, was improved to Olympic standard. It was open for more than a hundred years and greatly improved in 1881. The caretaker on the right is studiously aware of his responsibilities, while on the left a gentleman's servant waits with his towel for one of the Harrow schoolboys to take a dip. The pool was given up in 1984 and was then sold to the Swaminarayan Temple, but the project was not given planning permission (it was actually built later at Neasden).

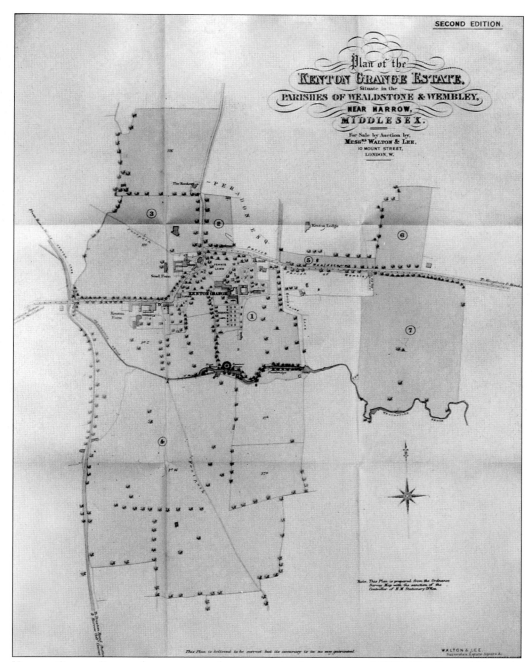

Kenton Grange Estate plan, as set out for prospective buyers around 1880. The line of the main road alongside the Grange was later straightened and the original road is now Woodgrange Avenue.

Kenton Grange was in the centre of Kenton village; it was built for John Lambert around 1805 (then known as Kenton Lodge but renamed by T.C. Gibson around 1853 as Kenton Grange). Various owners lived there during the remainder of the nineteenth century. About the time of the start of the First World War the Jeffress family (involved in tobacco) bought it and lived there until 1949, when it was up for sale and then bought by Wembley Council to be used as an old people's home. It is well hidden by trees from the Kenton Road and now houses the St Luke's Hospice, marvellously supported by local charities and by the mayors of Brent and Harrow.

Miniature railway in the grounds of Kenton Grange. The railway was created by the Jeffress family in the 1930s, who teamed up with railway enthusiast Henry Greenly. It must have been great fun for young and old alike.

Henry Cooper, the boxing champion, at the height of his pugilistic fame in the 1970s. He was visiting Kenton Grange at the time when it was on old people's home. He had been living in Ledway Gardens, Preston and helped in the family greengrocer's shop in the Ealing Road, Wembley.

Westfield House in Charlton Road pictured in 1959, prior to demolition. The house was built prior to the First World War. It was used as Kenton College by Alec Dalton. The site is now used by Kenton Evangelical church.

Chalkhill House, in the 1880s, was one of the larger mansions on the edge of Kingsbury. I believe the couple pictured are Henry Rawlings and his wife. He was from the family which made Rawlings mineral waters. (Is there something in Kingsbury which attracted soft-drink manufacturers? There were the Williams at Big Bush Farm, too!) It survived until the opening up of the district because of the creation of the British Empire Exhibition and the Wembley stadium in 1923-25 generated the same overwhelming demand for development which engulfed most of the area covered in this book, as elsewhere in suburban London. In the 1920s, an estate was built, marketed under the Metroland idiom, of bungalows with large gardens which were highly sought after. Close to Wembley Park station, it was a model of future commuter-style living. By the time many of the original families had reached retirement in the 1960s, Chalkhill was seen as ripe for redevelopment. The local council, not without some controversy, undertook this and a vast estate was built – in the new millennium, it is being rebuilt. One wonders what the inhabitants of the house in its leisurely Victorian days would have thought of the vast mass of concrete and brick which has now supplanted the house and carefully planted garden.

Four
Street Scenes

As we move closer to the middle of last century, the number of 'lost' buildings gets smaller. Now we enter 'Metroland' – that superb marketing creation of R.H. Selbie, the general manager of the Metropolitan Railway from 1908 to 1930, and his team – creating suburban homes serviced by railways, with consequential improvements to roads and bus routes. The field paths became high streets, the winding lanes were straightened and the trees were cut down to make way for street lamps.

As the illustrations reveal, horse-drawn carts were replaced by bicycles and they in turn by motor cars. Shopping parades line the principal roads, interspersed with railway stations, cinemas and public houses. The tarmacked streets are lined with red-brick semis and laburnums and limes, rather than elms and oaks. In the name invented by Ian Nairn, this is 'Subtopia'.

Kenton Road in 1933. Looking east, Kenton Lane is off to the left and Woodcock Hill is on the right. The shopping centre had only just been set up, but still looks as if it has been there for years. T.F. Nash who, with the Costins, was the co-creator of modern Kenton, built the shops, with flats above, forming Kenton Park Parade. The standard of street lighting is not what we expect today and you could park your car (if you had one, that is) wherever you liked.

Stag Lane, Kingsbury, in the 1960s. Looking north, Goldsmith Lane is on the left and the small shopping centre is in the middle distance, opposite Grove Park. On the right is Roberts Court, a council-built old people's home, named after the famous nineteenth-century general (see Chapter Two).

Springfield Mount, part of Laing's 1920s estates in Kingsbury. It is on the steeply rising east side of Wakeman's Hill; the name itself describes the location. Yet again there is the obligatory Kingsbury Council gas lamp.

Springfield Mount in 1931. The houses are rushing up and the haystacks won't remain long, stolidly waiting to be used for cattle feed. Kingsbury was for centuries a great source of hay for the capital, until, as elsewhere, the rise of motor traffic reduced and eventually eliminated the use of horse-drawn vehicles. One of the advertisements reads: 'This is one of the many estates developed by [Laing] in which full use is made of GAS LIGHT AND COKE COMPANY service. Each house is fitted with points for cooker, water heater, wash copper and gas fires. A coke boiler provides an alternative means of hot water supply and is ignited by a gas poker.'

Kingsbury Circle from the western side. These are typical 1930s suburbs, where Kingsbury and Kenton meet. The Prince of Wales public house is on the left with the 'Bandwagon' next to it – it achieved a degree of notoriety for a short while in the 1970s as a noisy disco. Further on, the mock-Tudor style for shops and flats above lead the eye to Kingsbury station.

Kenton Park Dairy. Mr J. Brazier and his dairymen are ready to serve the customers of Kenton in the early 1930s. Kenton Park Dairy had a range of vehicles for the delivery of milk from their farm at Kenton Lane (see Chapter One), including motorbike, handcarts and van – all very smart, too.

50

Church Lane, Kingsbury, *c.* 1929. Looking north to Kingsbury Road, the grocery shop is on the corner of Queensbury Road. The pillar box is now about fifty yards further north and on the left flats like Elvin Court (named after the leading light of Wembley Stadium – Sir Arthur Elvin) will be built. Note Kingsbury Council's sparse street lighting – a recurrent feature in these pictures!

Boycroft Avenue, Kingsbury

Street after street of houses like these in Boycroft Avenue strode across the one-time farmlands of Kingsbury and other London suburbs. This view looks north to Lewgars Avenue, with Stewart Close first left, pictured on a late afternoon in 1930 or thereabouts.

Roe Green in 1930. Horses graze undisturbed and it is still an open space today, though between then and now a swimming pool was built, opened, used by Olympic champions for training, then demolished – and may again arise.

Buck Lane in 1931, once again with the essential Kingsbury Council gas lamp.

Kingsbury Road in the late 1930s, with Station Parade at Nos 620-630. It is a road with character, since it knows it is the hub of a busy, thrusting new suburb. By the 1960s, it was well established and heavily trafficked (but no yellow lines or parking zones yet). There were many commuters from Kingsbury station and the line of shops showed little change over the years, apart from the style of shop-front. The pace of change continues – the now omni-present McDonald's has its restaurant here, as well as new-style public houses, converted from previous shops.

The Duck in the Pond c. 1910. This inn is on Upper Kenton Lane at the junction with Mountside (at the furthest stretch of my 'territory' of Kenton). What the policemen are doing there, we can only guess. It was rebuilt and is still today a most handsome pub.

Campden Crescent, charmingly suburban, with one of the Gloucestershire Northwick village names.

Prefabs in Pilgrims' Way in the 1950s. The end of the Second World War saw an enormous demand for housing, some of which was valiantly met by converting some aircraft manufacturers into house builders and using wartime techniques to turn out hundreds of pre-fabricated one-storey houses. They were meant to last ten years, but some had a much longer life. These, on the edge of the Fryent Open Space, called Pilgrims' Way, were among the last to go in Wembley. Brent Council decided in 1968 to use part of the site for a permanent housing development, giving an undertaking that there would be no further encroachment on the green acres behind.

Five
The Developing Suburb

The twenties and thirties in the suburbs are now revealed as a time of heightened expectations untrammelled by fear of any war. Life might have been hard at work, but at play tennis and golf were just round the corner. Everyone did their shopping in equally handy rows of shops where the staff were only too ready to serve, and estate agents just fell over each other in their eagerness to offer just the right house for you.

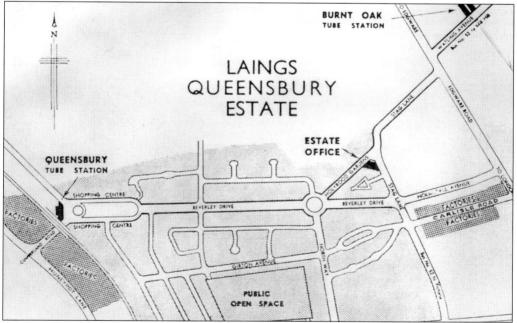

Springfield Parade, on Edgware Road near Wakeman's Hill Avenue, in the 1960s. The shopping centre was built by (Sir) John Laing as part of a planned development for a complete community, as at Queensbury. It was named after Springfield House, on Edgware Road. The Laing estate office was at No. 1 in the Parade. As their advertisement modestly said: 'It serves a thickly populated district and is a thriving and attractive shopping centre typical of the result of Laing's thoughtful and far-seeing Estate planning'. This estate was the first he built after arriving in London from the Lakelands – the road names: Crummock, Lodore, Ennerdale and so on recall his childhood home.

These two views of the brand-new Queensbury station, from the London Transport collection, were taken a few months apart in 1934.

Queensbury, late 1920s. As Kingsbury began to develop rapidly – towards the end of the 1920s – an enterprising builder, Mr Percy Edwards, saw an opportunity for a big housing development. He hit on a brainwave, a competition to name the new area, but in fact he did not like the replies and came up with his own solution – 'Queensbury', in respectful imitation of the larger district. His building area was around Queensbury Circle; he also built the Summit Estate in Kingsbury. A short distance away to the south was the new Metropolitan Railway station, which naturally took the newly adopted name. Next to it, was the shopping centre and part of the housing estate. Laing was the building contractor. There were to be 1,000 houses and the shopping centre, as well as a cinema. Again, modestly, John Laing called it: 'the most beautiful Station Square in London'.

Queensbury station, seen here first as the early building development by London Transport (the London Passenger Transport Board had taken over in 1933) and then opened in 1934 to meet the rapidly expanding suburb. Henry Neale was one of the larger engineering contractors who undertook the project. It was on the Metropolitan extension from Wembley Park to Stanmore through Kingsbury. There had been some argument with de Havilland about the right of way for the new line but in the end good sense prevailed.

The Harrow Masonic Centre was originally, in Spencer Churchill's ideal plan, a sports centre called, in Greek style 'The Palaestra'. The Northwick Park Tennis Club then built its magnificent pavilion in the 1920s, which flourished for many frenzied years, before being taken over as the centre for the Harrow District Masonic Association. One of the lodges originally met at the Rest Hotel – yet another local connection.

The Masonic Centre as seen in the 1980s, with ample space for cars in this modern day and age!

Woodcock Dell Estate, Northwick Park.

Only 8 miles from Baker Street, having the benefit of being within easy reach of 2 Stations on the Metropolitan Railway, Preston Road and Northwick Park, with an unexcelled service of fast electric trains to and from Baker Street and The City.

THE Estate is actually the site of the old Woodcock Dell Farmhouse and nearby is Kenton and the old hamlet of Preston. There are many facilities for outdoor recreation, including Tennis Courts. The golf course at Northwick Park is immediately adjacent, and others are within easy reach, with the large Sports Ground of Messrs. Selfridge directly adjoining the Estate, adding much to preserve the attractive features of the open countryside.

Schools, Churches and Shops are within easy distance.

The Estate comprises some 8½ acres with about 2,800 ft. frontage of land ready for immediate building.

Beautiful sites are now available from £150 suitable for the erection of Semi-detached or Detached Houses, and a single plot or large sections can be taken up on exceptional terms of purchase.

For further particulars and a plan of the Estate apply :—

H. GIBSON,

Metropolitan Railway Surplus Lands Committee,

General Offices : **Baker Street Station, N.W.1.**   Welbeck 6688.

Metroland advertisement for the Woodcock Dell Estate. When the Metropolitan Railway was extended from Baker Street to Harrow in 1879, the far-seeing chairman, Sir Edward Watkin, recognized that they had bought more land than was actually needed for the railway itself. One such example is Wembley Park. Slowly at first but then with great commercial skill, they coined and promoted the idea of Metroland – the utopia of suburbia – along the line of the railway out to and way beyond Harrow. On one of the farms of the Northwick demesne, the Woodcock Dell Estate was developed.

Kenton Road, outside Kenton Station, looking east, in the 1930s. The Rest Hotel (not yet 'The Travellers' Rest') is on the left. The suburb is near the beginning of its creation as a thriving district. Fifty years later, Sainsbury's were to win a long drawn-out planning battle to develop a new superstore behind the station, and the bridge was rebuilt and widened.

Costin advertise their houses on the Woodcock Dell estate and on the slightly more elegantly built Lyon Farm Estate at Preston, the land having once belonged to one of the founders of Harrow School, John Lyon.

MR. F. COSTIN.   MR. C. E. COSTIN.

F. & C. COSTIN Ltd.

Builders of Modern High-class Homes

KENTON & PRESTON
MIDDLESEX

Telephone : WORDSWORTH 2244 (3 lines)

NOTE.—This Booklet is issued for the guidance only of prospective purchasers and to give, as nearly as possible, particulars of the type of house enquired for, but is in no way to form any basis for or part of a contract. We reserve the right to make any alteration in details or construction at any time.

Choosing a House

BUYING a house is, even to the most matter-of-fact of us, an undertaking of the utmost importance. When the selection of a house is finally made in which one is to live perhaps the major portion of one's life, one necessarily makes a decision which has very far-reaching effects on health, happiness and prosperity. Obviously then, one cannot make the decision too carefully.

The aim of this booklet is of course to induce you to select a "COSTIN" HOUSE. We propose to try and do this, not by high-tension salesmanship, but by laying before you the plain unvarnished facts concerning "COSTIN" HOUSES and the estates on which they are built.

Let us begin by placing before you the salient features of

"Costin" Houses.

Now, no matter what it is you are purchasing, if you are wise you will first want to know something of the firm with whom you propose to deal. Let us, therefore, introduce ourselves.

OUR REPUTATION.—We are actual Builders, Contractors and Estate Developers operating on a large scale. The Directors being members of a family who have been builders for three generations. Moreover, we have a firmly established reputation among important Architects and Surveyors under whom we have carried out important contracts. Every department has a fully equipped staff we also have our own selling organization.

MATERIALS.—The choice of materials is of the utmost importance in building, and every house-buyer should satisfy himself of the quality of the materials employed in the building of the house he purchases. As will be evident from the following notes only materials of reliable quality are used in the building of every "Costin" House.

FOUNDATIONS.—The foundations of "Costin" Houses are of washed river ballast and best Portland cement, reinforced with steel rods. This is a point, the importance of which cannot be over-estimated. Most present-day houses are erected on inferior foundations, with disastrous result in course of time.

The estate developers, Fred & Charles Costin. Their office on Kenton Road literally held the key for many young couples trying to buying their first home. They began the transformation of Kenton from farmland to suburb with the 170-acre Northwick Park Estate, following E.G. Spencer Churchill and naming the roads after villages in the original Northwick Park area at Blockley in Gloucestershire.

The South Kenton and Preston Park Residents' Association, like others in the district, started in 1936 more for social activities and then became involved in local, non-partisan, campaigning for safer roads, protection of the environment and so on. Here they celebrate their twenty-first anniversary with a party at Preston Park School on 6 July 1957 – the children enjoy showing off in fancy dress!

Residents fought a long battle to get London Transport to build a subway under the railway at South Kenton station to give passengers easier access to and from the estates on each side. Here the Mayor of Wembley, Alderman Francis Pratt, triumphantly reads the notice proclaiming 'Welcome to South Kenton' on 29 February 1964. The Deputy Mayor, Alderman Thomas Gornall, wearing a hat, can just seen behind the Mayor.

The route to the golf club from the station. The new suburban dwellers thrived on sport – tennis and golf especially. However, the enthusiasm did not last long. By the middle of the twentieth century, change was about to take place and on the site was to be built the Harrow Technical College and then Northwick Park Hospital – the obvious name for the state-of-the-art hospital. It was the decay of all-round security in recent years that caused the closure of many of these extra station exits and entrances, another sad reflection on modern society's attitudes.

The South Kenton and Preston Park Residents' Association celebrate their Silver Jubilee on 13 January 1962 with a dinner at the Century Hotel, Wembley (now demolished for a housing development). Alderman Ted Lee, the Mayor of Wembley, is addressing the gathering. To the left is Mrs Keutgen, the wife of the President, Mr Gerhard Keutgen who is on Mr Lee's right and then Mrs Lee, the Mayoress.

This is how it was planned to be – the new housing on Woodcock Dell and Woodcock Hill Estates. New roads to be laid out, the link to the railway and the main roads – it is all there. Selfridge's sports ground was acquired by the council and renamed John Billam Sports Ground, after a chairman of the Middlesex County Council Education Committee and also a past mayor of Wembley. After many years of council activity, it was sold to a private group.

Shorts Croft. This is one of the roads in Roe Green Village. In the First World War, Kingsbury developed a thriving aircraft industry to support the new military aerodrome at Hendon (see Chapter Nine). The need for houses for the workers led to the building of a model village, designed by Sir Frank Baines. It was actually and unsurprisingly finished *after* the war was over, in 1918. However, its pleasing designs, friendly neighbourhood and compact layout have made it a delight ever since. It is now protected by a Conservation Order.

Roe Lane and Goldsmith Lane in the Village. This house is at the junction of Roe Lane and Goldsmith Lane, with the Tyler's Building (as it is now called) of Kingsbury High School in the background.

The Roe Green estate in the 1920s. It has retained its feeling of a secluded corner of Kingsbury, while not seeming cut off from the rest of the district.

Roe Lane showing the estate in its original layout – friendly, calm, neighbourly.

Brave new Kingsbury in 1932. Compare this with the 1960s scene on p. 50. Again, the essential Kingsbury Council lamp-post is in evidence. This photograph dates from a short time after the Metropolitan extension opened. The estate developer is Prince & Co. and some of the houses in Crundale Avenue are in the background.

In 1922, a Co-operative Society van stops outside the shop in Stag Lane. It has come from Willesden to serve the Roe Green Estate. It is quite an event – everyone, including children, has come to watch. The shops are still there, opposite Grove Park.

Local advertising in Kenton. The enterprising school magazine at Priestmead in 1938 picks up support from local enterprises – cars and gardens, the essentials of 1930s suburban life. The magazine was produced under the direction of the head teacher, Miss Gladys Driver, who was herself educated at Brondesbury and Kilburn Girls' School, in the early years of the last century.

FREEHOLD

£785

Total Deposit

£50

NO LAW COSTS
NO ROAD CHARGES

AT **KENTON**
THE IDEAL SUBURB

£1 · 1 · 11 PER WEEK

ONLY 9 MILES FROM CHARING CROSS
15 MINUTES FROM BAKER ST.
Served by three Railways.
MET., L.M.S. AND BAKERLOO.
LOWEST RATES AND TAXES
IN MIDDLESEX.
Electricity 4d. per unit.
EXCELLENT SHOPPING
FACILITIES,
SCHOOLS AND
CHURCHES.

Low Season
Ticket
Rates.

These semi-detached houses with garage space are distinctive, artistic and modern, and are now offered on the best terms available in London. Soundly constructed, with double slate damp course, lead flashings, close boarded roof, English tiles, Crittall steel windows.

Accommodation : 2 good reception rooms, 3 bedrooms, roomy tiled kitchen, with Ideal boiler gas copper, glass-fronted dresser. Tiled bathroom with built-in bath. Separate W.C.

Good gardens, close boarded fences. Houses back on to open space.

Also larger types **£835, £895 and £995**

EDWARDS

Telephone: HARROW 3164.
STATION APPROACH **KENTON**

Edwards (but not the Edwards who devised Queensbury – see p. 57) was one of the estate agents who realized the potential of the new Metroland suburbs and, in the late 1920s, was offering houses at the eye-catching figure of £1 1s 11d per week. Who could resist the call to live in the 'ideal suburb', in charming, well-designed houses close to the railway, schools and churches?

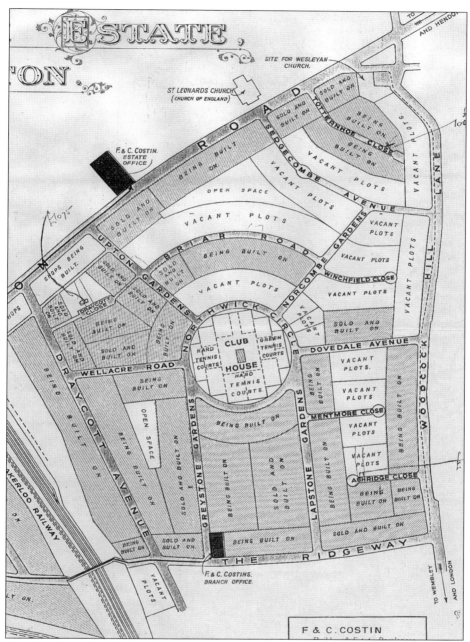

The Northwick estate was developed in the 1920s, largely by F. & C. Costin, a firm of local builders who were part of the 'big three' Wembley developers along with Comben & Wakeling and John Laing. The road names, such as Upton, Lapstone and Draycott, are connected with the Northwick estate in Gloucestershire. This is the eastern half of their publicity map. It must have been very tempting for prosperous young couples to pick their vacant plot and, for £1,050, have the house of their dreams built. The reference to St Leonard's church is the one that was replaced by St Mary's (see Chapter Seven), while the Club House is now the Harrow Masonic Centre.

Northwick Park Station, on the Metropolitan Line, opened in 1923. It was actually called Kenton and Northwick Park for a short while, until 1933. Its existence proclaimed the arrival of the suburb, now complete with its own transport link.

The Kingsbury Horticultural Association's new premises were opened in 1969 by the Mayor, Alderman Arthur Sharpe, with the Mayoress; on the left of the table are, Alderman Trevor Davies (who had preceded Alderman Sharpe as Mayor) and his wife Nancy.

Six

Beer and Flicks

It was the Roman poet Juvenal who declared that all the people of the city wished for was free food and entertainment – bread and circuses. The modern equivalents might be pubs and cinemas; they are hardly free, but they are just as desired. The inn became, and remained over hundreds of years, part of the living heart of every village, along with the church and the manor house.

The cinemas, for a short period from 1930 to 1960, nearly superseded the pubs as the place of resort for the family. That was until television and a changing way of life in the late twentieth century nearly killed them off. Certainly, in Kenton and Kingsbury with no cinemas still in existence, they are shadows only, recalling transient past glories, one-time palaces of fantasy.

This montage shows Kenton's most famous hostelry in some of its stages from country pub to local landmark. Clockwise from top left: 1902, 1906, 1900s, 1960s and (centre) 1930s. The 1900s picture (bottom right) shows the guests reflecting the pub's languorous name. The boaters and Edwardian dress suggest a summer's afternoon; the bicycles could belong to members of the Clarion Cycling Club – there are two notices headed 'Bicycle' to the right of the doorway. The Three Horse Shoes became the Rest in 1902, shortly before the top left picture was taken, and developed as a delightful place for country excursions. In the 1906 view there is still no Kenton station to serve commuters, but by the 1930s the inn found itself at the heart of the new suburbia; the mock Tudor style of the centre view is in keeping with many buildings nearby. It became the largest public house in Middlesex. By the 1960s, there is no car parking allowed on the forecourt but the pub is just as popular as it is today. A little later, some big food shops considered buying the pub in order to build a superstore; fortunately, they did not succeed. However, the attempt spurred Sainsbury's to try to build on the Kenton station goods yard, which they eventually succeeded in doing after a long battle with residents.

The Plough at Kingsbury, c. 1900. One of the most popular pub names is found adorning two pubs within a mile or two of each other along the road from The Hyde at Hendon to Tyburn Lane in Harrow. This scene, from the 1920s, reveals the old-style weather-boarding of the country village pub, which at that time it still was. However, it is not the village elders sitting outside, nor is it horses they ride, but bicycles. The house claimed to be over 800 years old, but there are no records of its existence before 1748. The old building was demolished in 1932 to be replaced by something more modern.

Another view of the Plough.

Wedding at the Plough, *c*. 1900. Mr Henry Johnson, the licensee of the inn, gives away his daughter to Mr Alfred Lincoln.

The Plough at Kenton, two miles away from the Kingsbury Plough, was also first licensed in the eighteenth century. These pictures show the kind of change that repeated itself everywhere as different periods and standards prevailed. In the hamlet of Kenton, the pub and the Grange formed the centrepieces of the community throughout the nineteenth century. The earlier picture (above) still shows a country-style pub, in the 1920s. The later version (below) shows it floodlit after it was rebuilt in the 1930s, to attract the smart set – the proprietor was H.H. Harrison. In the older scene, the houses in the distance on the right are in Woodgrange Avenue and the building through the trees on the left is Kenton Grange (see Chapter Three).

The Kingsbury Veterans' Club. Based at the old Sutherland Mansion (which was set up as the Veterans' Club after the war by Wembley Council), they are pictured in 1969, cheered on their outing by the Mayor, Alderman Arthur Sharpe.

The Green Man (complete with horse trough), Slough Lane, Kingsbury, c. 1910. This is another pub name of great antiquity widely distributed throughout the country. Like many others in the district, it was rebuilt (in the 1930s), to meet the changing tastes of its customers and to better serve the growing new communities that came with the expanding suburbs.

The Odeon in Kingsbury Road was designed by A.P. Sharkey and built in 1934 on the site that had once been Dr Arthur White's notorious piggeries at Gore Farm (whose name is redolent of the old Hundred – see Chapter One). When the cinemas in Brent closed down one by one, Harrow kept the flag flying; two cinemas recently reopened in Willesden. This one, demolished in 1972, became the site of a Sainsbury's branch. When that closed, it was taken over by Aldi.

The Savoy cinema, Burnt Oak, c. 1936. Like a number of cinemas, it changed its name before eventually closing due to competition from television. In the 1950s, John Godfrey was the manager and the admission prices were: stalls, 1s 3d, 1s 9d and 2s 3d; circle, 2s 9d, 3s 6d. This cinema became an Essoldo, which company had several other cinemas in the area. By the 1970s it had become a Mecca casino.

The Odeon in Kenton Road was built to a design by George Coles, who designed many on the Odeon circuit, and opened in 1933. Sadly, its destruction to make way for a Waitrose store made more news than its short life as a cinema.

The interior of the Regal, Burnt Oak, c. 1936. This was the luxury of the picture palace; it was sometimes satirized but was always a refuge from harsh reality, a factory of dreams.

The Old Welsh Harp in 1902. This was one of the most famous inns in London, especially under the auspices of William Warner in the latter part of the nineteenth century. He laid out a racecourse in the fields nearby, supported fishing in the reservoir and organized concert parties with some of the top names of the day. The pleasure gardens became so popular with Londoners (music hall songs were even written about them!) that the Midland Railway opened a station simply to cater for the customers attracted there. In the distance is the Upper Welsh Harp inn. Sad to relate, fashions changed and the place declined in popularity. In the 1970s it got in the way of building the gigantic Staples Corner flyover and was pulled down, quite unnecessarily, I am told, as the space it occupied is still derelict land.

Seven

A Variety of Faiths

St Andrew's is said to be the second oldest church in Middlesex, although there are some experts who believe it may not have been erected until the twelfth century. The Domesday Book lists a priest with a quite large holding of land. The style of part of the building is Saxon (with some Roman material), but this is not firm evidence of pre-Norman construction. By the middle of the thirteenth century, it had become the church of the St John's Hospitallers on their Freren (i.e. brothers – later written as Fryent) estate. In the Great Plague of 1349, the village population reduced by about half and those left fled to Kingsbury Green. By the 1880s, the parish was in some disarray and threatened with closure. A new church was built in the north, Holy Innocents, while for a time St Andrews became the church of Neasden and Kingsbury. By the 1930s the new developing suburb demanded a new, larger church.

An early print of St Andrew's church, Kingsbury, 1822.

The new St Andrew's.

The church as it was once in Wells Street, Marylebone, before being transplanted, stone by stone to Kingsbury in 1934. The relocated church stands on its hilltop next to its predecessor. Just to the north, one of the roads is named Wells Drive in recognition of the church's former home.

Holy Innocents, early 1900s. It was built in 1884 in Kingsbury Road, near the northern end of Church Lane (which thus came to link the two Kingsbury churches). Following a row about old St Andrews, it was decided to build a new parish church for Kingsbury and the site on Kingsbury Road was chosen for Holy Innocents. This is a familiar country scene but the usual Kingsbury Council gas lamp is there!

Holy Innocents, perched on the slope of the highest part of Wembley, was built to a design by the famous church architect William Butterfield in 1884 (though it is not one of his most distinguished buildings) when Hyde Lane (Kingsbury Road) was still a country road.

The Kenton Methodist church, 1960. The site for the church was included in the estate plans by Costins; it started in what is now the church hall in 1929.

A picture by the local photographer Kuno Reitz shows the laying of the foundation stone. The present building opened on 15 September 1937.

This inside shot recalls a broadcast in August 1960 by Independent Television, with Revd Ronald Pearce in the pulpit.

St Leonard's, Kenton Road. This wooden building opened in 1927 to meet the needs of the growing Anglican community in the new Kenton.

St. Mary's Church, Kenton Road.

St Mary's church, Kenton Road, replaced St Leonard's in 1936. The money to build it came from the sale of St Mary the Virgin's church in Charing Cross, which is why the name was changed from St Leonard's. It became, in the 1950s, the church of what was regarded as the largest parish in the diocese of London (in medieval times the parish of St Mary's at Harrow-on-the-Hill was the largest parish in England). On a rather humdrum suburban road, the building, designed by J.H. Gibbons, stands out for its architectural simplicity and charm. The slightly later picture shows how charming it is in a setting of trees and greenery.

The Greek church of St Pantelimion, which took over the Holy Spirit, rededicated in its own Orthodox style. Here, in 2000, the Mayor of Harrow, Cllr Keeki Thammaiah, is greeted by Fr Anastasios Sallapatas.

Kenton Synagogue, in Shaftesbury Avenue, showing a general view of the interior and the sacred areas – the 'Bima' or altar, and the Ark, housing the Scrolls of the Law or Torah. The first service was held in August 1958 by Cyril Harris and the building was consecrated by Dayan Meyer Steinberg on 13 September 1959.

In October 1932 the Mission church of the Holy Spirit, at the eastern end of Kenton Road was dedicated by the Bishop of London in order to help parishioners of St Leonard's which had become overcrowded. In 1994, it had become redundant and, as is happening repeatedly nowadays, another faith – the Greek Orthodox – was willing to take over.

The patron saint of the church.

Kingsbury Baptist church, which opened in 1931. The building was designed by C.W.B. Simmonds of Willesden, who undertook many commissions in Willesden and in Wembley. This student gathering, outside the church in Slough Lane in 1953 shows the strength of the church in attracting young people. Seated in the front are Margaret Gee, Peter Saunders, Revd Walter Macdonald and Marian Leaper.

The Bishop of London attends the consecration of the new church in 1936. He is pictured here knocking at the West Door.

Harrow and Wembley Progressive Synagogue. It was founded in 1947, as the Wembley Liberal Synagogue, securing a site in Preston Road on which it has steadily built and rebuilt as the congregation enlarged. This is the Consecration Service for the first permanent building, held on 5 September 1954. The chairman, Max Salter is on the left, together with Vice-President A.L. Ansell (with buttonhole), the Mayor of Wembley, Alderman Arthur Edmond and the Mayor of Harrow, Alderman W.R. Cowen OBE, and Philip Rigal, vice-chairman. On the left is a charming photograph from the wedding of the synagogue's first minister, Revd Vivian Simmonds to Theresa, who survived him until April 2000.

The Brent Sikh Temple in Kingsbury. An old faith is reborn on a former Brent Council depot site (above). The completion of the building of this temple is now (in 2001) well under way, supported by the Sikh Mayor of Brent in 1988, Mr H.S. Wadhwa, and now by leaders of the community including Mr A.S. Hoonjan.

The opening of Harold Poster House on Kingsbury Circle (the building has since undergone different uses and is now a hotel). This is the dedication to Mr Harold Poster in November 1977, who was a long-time worker for the Jewish National Fund. The Chief Rabbi, Dr Jakobovits, dedicated the building and the presentation was made by Dr (later Sir) Rhodes Boyson, the MP for the area. Sadly, Mr Poster died in the following year at the age of sixty-six.

St Cuthbert's at the southern end of Northwick Park, a clean, well-designed building. Here the Bishop of London is at the consecration in 1956 with the Mayor of Wembley, Cllr T.C. Wardle and the Deputy Mayor, Cllr L.J. Sullivan, their wives and the town clerk, Mr Kenneth Tansley.

Father (later Canon) John O'Callaghan at a reception in the Roman Catholic church of St Sebastian and St Pancras in Hay Lane in the 1970s. He is seen here with (clockwise from left): Tricia and Maria Freeman (daughters of the caretaker), Rita Mascarenhas, -?- (in background), Father O'Callaghan, Tricia Venning, Cecil Brooks Mills, Mr O'Neill, Rita Leonard, -?-, -?-, Mr Ruth. A small church had been opened close to Haydon House in 1926 and was gradually added to until it became the large church seen today. The Parish Hall was named in Father O'Callaghan's honour after his death in 1981.

The Convent of the Visitation on the side of Harrow Hill and on Harrow Manor land, in the early twentieth century. The site had been acquired by the Catholic diocese and now houses St George's Catholic School and the private Clementine Churchill Hospital.

Eight

In the Morning to School and After ...

Aerial view of Roe Green looking south, *c*. 1960. Pictured are the Tylers' Croft boys' and girls' Secondary Schools (which are now part of Kingsbury High School); the curved wings are clearly seen in the centre while Fryent Open Space stretches away to the top of the picture. It's possible to make out Kingsbury swimming pool, while in the foreground are the fields of Grove Park Mansion where, later, Roberts Court Old People's Home and two special schools were to be built.

Priestmead School in 1981. It opened in 1935 to serve the rapidly growing estates in this part of Kenton.

Oliver Goldsmith School, Kingsbury, opened in 1938. It was named after the famous author of *She Stoops to Conquer* who lived for a few years in on Hyde House Farm. An outbuilding known as Shell Cottage still survives, a few hundred yards from the school along the Kingsbury Road. The building is similar in style to Priestmead, built by the Middlesex County Council Education Department.

Infant class at Oliver Goldsmith School in 1956.

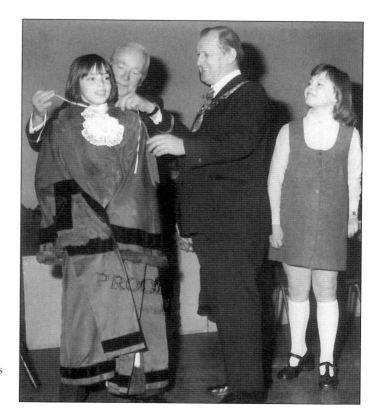

Alderman Bob Thompson shows off his mayoral robes to children at Oliver Goldsmith School. Bob Thompson was Mayor of Brent in 1974/75; here he is helped by his attendant, Bill Brown.

The Mayor of Brent, Alderman Bob Thompson, at Oliver Goldsmith School in 1975, tries his hand at rolling pennies down the chute of the model pool made by some of the pupils. Holding the pool is Simon Wells and looking on are Sarah Lax and Andrew Keogh, who presented a cheque for £300 to the Mayor for his 'Gemini' fund. The fund was in support of a swimming pool at the school for handicapped children at nearby Grove Park (that is the Brent Council school, not the one-time private preparatory school).

Oliver Goldsmith, a portrait of the man himself. He wrote his wonderful comedy *She Stoops to Conquer* and other works while staying with Robert Selby at Hyde House Farm on Hyde Lane, now Kingsbury Road. Perhaps the air of Kingsbury stimulated humour! (By Sir Joshua Reynolds – Courtesy the National Portrait Gallery, London)

Kingsbury County Grammar School, 1932. It was built by John Laing for £43,638. Kingsbury County Grammar, now Kingsbury High, went on to grow and when in 1967 the comprehensive system for secondary schools was introduced, it was linked with the two Tyler's Croft Schools and became the largest secondary school in Brent – which it has remained. There was a Kingsbury Board School was next to the Red Lion, in Kingsbury Road, from 1875 until bombed in the last war. Council flats now occupy the site.

Staff at Kingsbury County in 1932, led by the headteacher Dr A.G. Tracey.

Tyler's Croft School before its merger into Kingsbury High.

Kenmore Park School opened in 1938 in Kenton.

Mr H. Walker and staff at Kenmore Park School in 1956.

Celebrating life. The Queen's Silver Jubilee Festival in Harrow, 1977, at Kenmore Park Junior School.

Mount Stewart Junior School opened in 1952 to an expectant community.

The recently elected Member of Parliament for Bexley, Mr Edward Heath, was presciently invited to open the school, on 19 October 1953, by his colleague Eric Bullus, MP for Wembley North, on Mr Heath's left. The school was to benefit for many years under its new – and long to be exciting – head teacher, Mr Kenneth Rudge (on the right of the picture).

The school excelled at sports, here represented by the boys' football team of 1962/63 and the girls' netball team of 1983.

There was a fancy dress parade at Mount Stewart Junior School in 1960 with the centrepiece being a protest against the then Chancellor of the Exchequer, Mr Selwyn Lloyd, for his 15% tax.

Grove Park Preparatory School, Kingsbury, N.W.9.

Grove Park Mansion was turned into a boys' preparatory school from 1923 until the outbreak of the Second World War – these pictures show the elegant rooms converted for classroom use.

Eton Grove Open Space in the late 1950s. On the roundabout are the Limming children: Catherine, Stephen, Christine (who supplied the picture) and Caroline (with her head turned away).

Children in a class for seven-year-olds at Roe Green Junior School in 1954. In the middle, wearing his fancy hat and pointing a toy gun, is Stephen Limming.

'Stop me and buy one'. Walls Ice-Cream's famous slogan can be read on a tricycle that is brought to the gym (former coach-house) at Grove Park School in the 1920s.

Building Kingsbury Swimming Pool in 1938. This soon became an open-air paradise in the summer and a test bed for local Olympic swimmers like Judy Grinham. It is sad to relate that by the 1980s the zing had gone out of the local council's leisure activities and this pool, like many others, closed down for lack of support and also funding, and was filled in following a particularly tragic accident. At the beginning of the new Millennium, attempts were being made to reopen it with the help, in line with modern thinking, of a private backer.

Roe Green Junior School opened in 1932, with Mr Johnson as its first head. Like its senior neighbour, the school was built by Laing. The building was described as 'brick built and of fire-resisting construction generally, with reinforced concrete to the upper floors and staircases. Externally it is faced with multi-coloured bricks and roofed with red hand-made sand-faced tiles'. It is an ornament in the district. One of the largest primary schools in Brent, it shares a site with the infants' school.

Alderman Arthur Edmond, Mayor of Wembley in 1954 – busy, like all Mayors, this time making a presentation at Roe Green Junior School.

The staff of the school in September 1937. The head is Mr Johnson and pictured, from top left, clockwise are: Mr Barrow, Mr Crabb, Mr Colbeck, Mr Warrington, Mr Records, Mr Honley, Mr Corby, Mr Mackle, Mrs McMenamin, Miss Cobb, Miss Begley, Mr Johnson, Miss Ronketto (Senior Mistress), Miss Harrow and Miss Bateman.

Harrow schoolboys skate on the Ducker in the 1970s – they often went wild with joy at the alternative use of the swimming pool.

5th Kingsbury Guides in 1970 dressed up in 1919 style.

Kenton Synagogue Youth Club in 1968; they moved into their purpose-built youth centre across the road, in 1969.

Mr Dumain, in the garden of his house on Roe Green. This was once the Kingsbury Board school, later it was owned by Mrs Fox, who had a sweet-shop there – known as Fox's corner. All that is left to remind us of it is the delightful flowerbed at the corner with Kingsbury Road.

Staff of Harrow County Boys' School, 1945. The headmaster, in the centre, is Revd Randall Williams.

Opening of the Welsh Harp Sailing Base, 1963. The last Mayor of Wembley, Alderman Thomas Gornall, presides. The sailing base was set up on the north bank of the reservoir, at Birchen Grove. Thus, Wembley Council kicked off one of the exciting features of activity on the Welsh Harp. For a number of years, the Willesden regatta, then the Brent Regatta, took over the Welsh Harp for a day of joyous water sports.

View from the River

Boats on the Welsh Harp, *c.* 1900. Always a pleasure to watch them glide over the water, as we saw on Regatta days.

St Robert Southwell (1561-1595) was a Jesuit priest in the time of Queen Elizabeth I. He was caught up with the Bellamy family of Uxendon who became involved in the Babington plot to assassinate the Queen and replace her with Mary Queen of Scots. He was arrested at Uxendon Manor in 1592 and after torture was hanged at Tyburn. His subsequent martyrdom was recognized by the Catholic Church and he was canonised in 1970; his name was taken up for the Catholic Primary School in Slough Lane, Kingsbury. The school is linked to the parish of St Sebastian and St Pancras at Hay Lane, whose then priest, Father O'Callaghan searched successfully for a site for the school which was opened in 1967. (By W.J. Alais after C. Weld)

Edgar Mitchell, head of Kingsbury High School (1970 to 1988), is pictured in 1987 with the head boy and head girl and prefects. The system of pupil government seems to have dropped out of many modern comprehensive schools, but these senior students looked smart, armed with the distinguishing badge of authority.

A garden party organized by Mount Stewart Junior School in 1957, which was graced by the Rank film star, Shirley Eaton, who came from the Wembley area.

Grove Park Special School was established in 1928 in Willesden and, after several moves, was firmly located on the site of the former mansion in 1968. It celebrated its Diamond Jubilee on 6 December 1990 with a visit by the Queen (it was later than planned because of the sudden illness of Her Majesty on the very morning of the original date). She is seen here with Judy Edwards OBE, the head teacher, on her left and on the other side, the Chairman of the Governors, Mr Lawrie Nerva.

Nine
Work-a-Day

During the First World War, Kingsbury developed as a significant military aircraft manufacturing centre, supporting the major Hendon Aerodrome nearby. One of the most important firms that developed out of this activity was created by Geoffrey de Havilland, who started work with Airco (for whom he designed some of the most famous military aircraft of the war including the fighter, the DH4). At the end of the war, Airco folded, but Geoffrey de Havilland managed to put a team together. He built on the tiny works on the Stag Lane airfield, and went on to create one of the most prestigious firms in the aviation world, until it was absorbed by Hawker Siddeley and in turn by British Aerospace. In the 1930s the famous partnership of Jim Mollison and his wife Amy Johnson came to work for them.

De Havilland – from small beginnings in 1923.

The Stag Lane entrance to the fully developed de Havilland works, in 1948.

A DH aircraft touches down at the landing field in 1923.

Sir Geoffrey de Havilland and his team in 1952.

Cricket team from de Havilland at Stag Lane in the late 1940s. Bottom right is Stan Bolch and behind him is Ernest Limming.

Amy Mollison learning to fly at the London Aeroplane Club in Stag Lane, and Jim and Amy on tour (below).

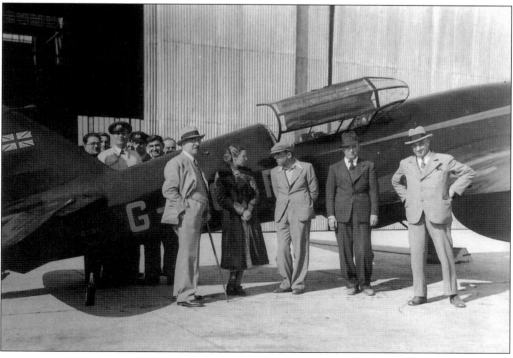

King George V and Queen Mary visit Airco during the First World War. This would have been a great morale booster.

One of the largest firms on the Kingsbury industrial estate was the Aircraft Manufacturing Company, usually known as Airco. In 1916 they took over Grove Park Mansion as their offices and planes flew from the park grounds. Workers are seen catching the 66 tram from Acton to Edgware (which is a mile or so to the north).

Kingsbury House had been rebuilt in the mid-nineteenth century. It was used during the First World War by Ernest Barningham and the Kingsbury Aviation Company – one of a number of industries which made the area a centre for military aircraft manufacturing at that momentous time: part of Kingsbury's amazing aviation history. It was demolished in 1926 when the site was taken over by the motor car firm, Vanden Plas (see Chapter Nine). It is now the Express Dairy Depot.

Vanden Plas – an aerial view of the hangars in which they carried out their motorcar work. They took over Kingsbury House, which had been the site of Kingsbury aviation. Kingsbury Road is bottom right and Church Lane at the top.

In the foreground are the factories of the Kingsbury Trading Estate along Kingsbury Road, with Church Lane on the right and Silver Jubilee Park beyond. On the left the southern part of Kingsbury stretches away in the distance.

Blackbird Garage in the 1930s. A corner of Blackbird Farm on Blackbird Hill was adapted for a more commercial use.

Kingsbury Motors in the 1960s. One of the many small firms that thrived along the Kingsbury Road.

The coach house at Kingsbury Manor, where John Logie Baird carried out early experiments in television.

John Logie Baird, a sculpture by Donald Gilbert. Baird carried out some of his early experiments in television in an outbuilding at Kingsbury Manor. The plaque from Wembley Council proudly recalls this work. There is also a memorial stone nearby, placed by the Wembley History Society, commemorating the erection of the mast used for the reception of the first television signals from the continent. Between 1928 and 1930, Baird rented this part of Kingsbury Manor, erected masts and received the first television signals from Berlin. The first combined sight and sound transmission was in March 1930. Remains of the foundations can still be seen. (Courtesy of the National Portrait Gallery, London)

'Here stands Northwick Park Hospital'. In the remains of Northwick Park Golf Club a solitary tree awaits its fate before the builders arrived to create the new hospital.

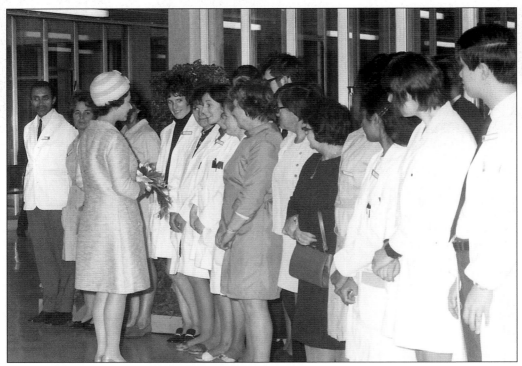

Queen Elizabeth meets staff of the new Northwick Park Hospital on the opening day, a nice change, for a few moments, from the more serious formalities.

When the site for the hospital was under debate, the clinching argument was that Northwick Park was on the playing fields of Harrow School – 'settled' said the chairman, an Old Etonian! And so, the long-held dream of a hospital on the land once owned by Lord Northwick came to shuddering realization when building work started in 1966 as bulldozers moved in from the Watford Road. The first patients were admitted on 5 September 1970. Who else but Her Majesty should be called on to open the Northwick Park Hospital and Clinical Research Centre, which she did with her supreme charm and aplomb on 23 October 1970. Here on the platform with her are Margaret Thatcher MP, the Secretary of State for Education and Science (the latter part of her title justifying her presence), the Duke of Northumberland (in his role as chairman of the Medical Research Council, thus involved with the other half of the total concept), Sir Maurice Hackett (the chairman of the Regional Hospital Board), Dr Brian Thwaites, chairman of the Hospital Management Committee to whom the whole project would be handed over, and the Lord Bishop of Willesden, the Rt Revd Graham Leonard.

Acknowledgements

I record my deepest appreciation of the wonderfully generous help and advice given to me by Geoff Hewlett, the Brent historian of Kingsbury and Kenton, who has also loaned me many pictures from his personal collection; Ian Johnston and Bob Thompson of the Brent and Harrow Archives respectively went out of their way to help me; many individuals have been thanked directly. I particularly thank: David Tobert, Jack Chamberlain of the Wembley History Society, Jerry Wayne, Sharon Carr, Bryan Guess of British Aerospace Systems Archives, Rita Gibbs, the Harrow School Archivist, Wayne Flintham, Alice Flynn, St Luke's Hospice (Kenton Grange), Sunil Hirandani, Judith Hill, May White, Norma Aubertin-Potter, the Codrington Librarian at All Souls' College, Oxford, John Keutgen and Geoffrey Bray. Way beyond the call of duty and family was the work of our daughter Sue, whose skills and enthusiasm bore me along considerably – many thanks to her. Another special thanks is due to the retiring head of Kingsbury High School, Phillip Snell, and to Mr Michael Long who gave me access to their selection of Kingsbury's history. The head and staff of the schools pictured in this book and the head or staff of the religious institutions illustrated have all been generous of their time in finding material – but especially Fr David Sherwood and Judy Edwards OBE. If there are any omissions, my humble apologies.

The advice and experience of Katherine Burton and her colleagues at Tempus Publishing has made this a far better book than I first envisaged. If there are any errors, I must accept the blame – but please tell me.

Copyright of the following is gratefully recorded:
London Transport Museum
Derek Sherborne,
Victoria County History of Middlesex
Aerofilms
Harrow School Library
All Souls' College, Oxford
National Monument Record
National Portrait Gallery
The majority of the other images are from the Brent Local Archives, Harrow Library Archives or the Wembley History Society whose permission was so generously granted.